RESURRECTION

A Manual for Raising the Dead

Ben R. Peters

Resurrection: A Manual for Raising the Dead
© 2006 by Ben R. Peters

Published by
KINGDOM SENDING CENTER
P. O. Box 25
Genoa, IL 60135

www.kingdomsendingcenter.org
ben.peters@kingdomsendingcenter.org

ISBN: 0-9767685-9-3

Cover art by Robert Bartow ~ *www.bartowimages.com*
Cover design and book interior by *www.ChristianBookDesign.com*

Contents

Preface

Let's Raise the Dead

Let's raise the dead! Why not? We believe in the concept. It is Scriptural you know. Actually, the credibility of all orthodox Christianity undeniably rests and depends on the physical resurrection of the man known as Jesus of Nazareth. Hebrews 6:1-2 lists the resurrection of the dead as one of the six foundational doctrines of the church. Raising the dead is most certainly and undeniably in our DNA as Christians.

Jesus Himself raised at least three people from the dead, and many saints in Jerusalem rose from their graves when He died. Jesus also commanded his twelve disciples to raise the dead, and both Peter and Paul raised the dead. And today, Christians all around the world are raising the dead, especially in third world nations, but also in America and other western nations.

Two Old Testament prophets, Elijah and Elisha, raised the dead. Ezekiel saw a whole valley full of dry bones come to life and rise up to become a mighty army.

Paul declared to King Agrippa, "Why should it be thought incredible by you that God should raise the dead?" (Acts 26:8). That's a good question to ask the western church, where we see very few resurrections today. What is the big deal about raising the dead? Paul seemed to think that even King Agrippa should not have a hard time believing in the resurrection power of God.

Death can be a terrible thief that robs us of those we love, but resurrection life has been given to us to reverse the curse of death. Because we don't really understand life and death like we would like to, this little book will help us discover some valuable principles revealed in Scripture so that whatever kind of death has taken place, we will be in the best possible position to produce life and erase the sting of death.

We will be looking at the actual resurrection of physical bodies, but we will be seeking to apply the things we learn to other very important kinds of resurrections as well. I fully expect to see literal physical resurrections taking place before my eyes through faith in the living God, but I also want to see spiritual death reversed and resurrection life invade spiritual corpses.

Because miracles are designed by God to build faith in those who observe them, physical resurrections will do much to build the Kingdom of Heaven on this earth. Spiritual resurrections, however, will not only restore the relationships of wandering souls to Jesus, their Savior, but it will put wounded soldiers back into the battlefield and weary harvesters back into the ripened harvest fields.

Let's explore the possibilities. Can you imagine yourself happening on the scene of an accident where someone has just died? There is no pulse, no breath and the body is already getting cold and losing color. The other accident victims are either injured or in shock. There is no ambulance and no one else available to help but you. What would you do, besides call 911? Can you see yourself taking authority over death and bringing life back into the corpse? I know of one person who did. Perhaps after reading this book you will too.

Perhaps you know of a traditional church that had begun with spiritual life and belief in a powerful, living God. However, you are aware that it is now run by unbelievers who preach nothing but a social gospel. The services follow the traditional religious ritual and no one is ever saved, healed or delivered within its four walls. You know some people who attend there and feel bad for them, but you want to keep them as friends and don't want to make waves, so you never say anything.

Because of your expertise in your field of work, you are asked to speak to the church group on a Wednesday night. You are given the freedom to share whatever you would like related to the subject. You know that what they need to hear about is the reality of your personal relationship and life in Jesus. Can you believe that God is able to speak life into these dry bones? Can you believe that through the Holy Spirit you can open up the hearts of those who have been spiritually dead for some time? I trust that after reading this book you could.

Chapter 1

A Simple Game of Life and Death

"**I** got you; you're dead!" shouted Grant Howatt, my neighbor friend, who lived two doors down from my house. I obediently stopped in my tracks and waited anxiously for someone to touch me and let me back into the game.

Grant had just connected with the elastic canning jar sealer ring. We shot them like rubber bands, and my skinny left forearm was loaded with twenty or thirty of them. Fortunately, our moms only used them one time for canning and then they were discarded and became our favorite weapons of war. It was a war game that we loved to play in our little neighborhood where I grew up on Arthur Street, now named 106th Street, in North Battleford, Saskatchewan, Canada.

The rules of the game were simple. We divided up into two armies, chosen by two captains. The goal was to take out everyone on the other team before they could take our team completely out. If you hit someone with the sealer ring, they were dead until someone on their team touched them. If you got touched, you could come back to life and get back in the game again.

I hadn't thought much about those events until recently when I was teaching about prophetic ministry and the coming harvest. Suddenly an anointing came to share this story and the application was incredibly powerful to everyone, including myself.

As John Eldridge, the author of *Wild at Heart,* so powerfully teaches, life on earth is all about warfare. If we don't realize we are in a war, we won't understand life.

We have a very nasty enemy. We cannot overestimate his hatred for God and for us, His children. He is not restricted by any code of ethics or by the Geneva Convention. He comes to steal, kill and destroy. He has no mercy or compassion. The crueler he can be, the better he likes it. And he will get away with everything he can. He will break every rule that's not strictly enforced.

His Target

And who does he like to target? The answer is simple—he targets everyone made in the image of God.

He wants to take us down and take us out. He wants to put us all out of commission. He will attack you just because you are a living human being made in the image of God. But if you are a Christian, he will attack you with an even greater fury. As a Christian you have the life of Jesus shining through you, and you can't possibly hide it from him. He knows who you are, you are a definite threat to him and he wants to take you down for good.

His Strategy

Our enemy has a plan and a strategy. His plan is to take down every Christian armed with the power of resurrection life. Like the game we used to play in our neighborhood, he wants to hit us with something that will neutralize our power before we can neutralize his. He considers us armed and dangerous. But he knows that if he can hit us quickly and consistently, the chances are good that we will go down, become casualties of war and won't make too many problems for him thereafter.

What he really hates is when Christians use their resurrection power to bring back to life those he has already mortally wounded and taken out of the battle. When that happens, he puts the highest priority on taking out those who are reviving the others.

Our enemy has a lot of resources at his disposal. He has demon hoards, who know every evil tactic to use to set ambushes and traps, dig pits, snipe, throw hand grenades and drop bombs on unsuspecting believers. He can also use human vessels, including other Christians, to say or do the very thing that will bring us to a place of defeat and discouragement.

But what he can't stop is the power of love that brings life back to those who have been taken out by his evil tactics. Those who know how to find and touch the "down and out" Christians with the spirit of life can do incredible damage to the kingdom of darkness. Today, we are seeing a new kind of Christian being raised up. Instead of just looking for help when they need it for themselves or their friends and families, this new breed is looking for others that need a touch from God.

Armed with an unstoppable passion for the Kingdom of God and a powerful anointing, which has been accessed through intimacy with their King, this new breed is ready to do battle with the prince of darkness. They are spending time in the presence of Jesus and have downloaded His heart. Their hearts beat with His passion and purpose, and they want to raise up every wounded soldier that they possibly can, putting the Sword of the Spirit back in their hands.

These are the folks who totally frustrate and torment the forces of the kingdom of darkness. Every time they take down some believers, someone comes along and picks them up, which makes them even tougher to take down. In addition, they become resurrection life givers. They become more intimate with Jesus and soon they are bringing life to others who are down like they were.

This activity is very literally a matter of life and death. We are talking about the eternal life or eternal death that others will receive as the result of what we do or do not do in this realm. Every child of God that we can raise up to go to war for our King will be capable of carrying the gospel to others, while those who remain down and out of action will do little to rescue people from the deathtrap that the enemy has set for them.

Chapter 2

Who is Able to Raise the Dead?

First of all, let me make this disclaimer: I am very much aware that no human being can raise up a dead body by himself or herself. It is only God, Himself, that can raise the dead. Having acknowledged that, Jesus told His disciples to raise the dead. And with this understanding, we will refer to human beings raising the dead with the knowledge that it is God working through a human vessel as the point of contact.

What then are the qualifications necessary for someone to be able to raise the dead? Perhaps you are wondering if even reading this manual is a waste of your time. You might feel that since you were never called to be an apostle you are disqualified. Or perhaps, you carry with you some guilt or feeling of failure from the past that convinces you that raising the dead is way out of your league.

You may feel that your faith is far too weak, your church doesn't give you enough support or good teaching, or that someone else is much more qualified than you. You probably feel a bit dead yourself and in need of someone else bringing you back to life.

But please don't stop reading if you have one of the above responses. You may be surprised to find out that what you thought were the necessary qualifications are not what God is asking for. Instead, you might discover that God has chosen some of the most least likely candidates to do His work in this strategic period of history, which is "His Story."

We are going to deal with natural and spiritual resurrections as if they were almost the same thing, especially in this chapter. The natural is given to us by God to teach us about the spiritual. The same principles apply and supernatural power and authority is needed for both.

What You Don't Need to Raise the Dead?

1. First of all, you don't need a degree in theology to raise the dead. I don't think the pastor's wife I met in Mozambique had a theology degree, but she had raised at least four people from the dead. It is true that Paul was highly educated, but Peter was a fisherman, Elisha was a farmer, and Jesus was a carpenter.

2. Secondly, you don't need a position in the church

or an official title that says you are some kind of professional minister of the gospel. You only need to understand that God desires for every one of His children to be a "full-time" minister, even if they don't get any income for being one.

3. Thirdly, you don't need a pure, spotless past or a perfect present. You don't need to be a Bible scholar or one who has fasted forty days and forty nights without food or water. You can be a person with flaws and blemishes who still struggles with things like pride, anger and self-pity.

What You Do Need to Raise the Dead

Without sharing too much from the chapters to come, let me give some general requirements for those who would join the ranks of those who raise the dead.

1. First of all, God is looking for those who will give Him all the glory. He is looking for those who know they are not worthy or holy enough to do anything for God without His grace and mercy flowing through them. God used a donkey to prophesy and dead bones to raise up a dead man. He can use anyone, but He will always choose a humble vessel before a proud one.

2. Secondly, God will use someone who is used to listening to His voice. The people God raises from the dead are usually those who died prematurely, and that often happens without much warning. Accident fatalities

that happen on the highway would fall into that category. Sudden fatal illnesses are another example.

People who are not used to listening for God's still small voice will not be tuned in to hear Him encourage them to pray for a dead person. But those who practice listening to His voice will be in a much better position to hear and to clearly recognize that it is indeed God speaking and not just their own mind.

3. Thirdly, God will use someone with an obedient servant heart and the courage to do whatever God asks them to do. Praying for a dead body is not the socially acceptable thing to do and sometimes there will be many close relatives and friends in your presence. When God speaks to us to do something embarrassing, we need to be willing to be a fool for Christ. As Heidi Baker said to a friend of mine: "How will we raise the dead if we never pray for anyone dead to be raised? They are not going to come into our living room. We need to be bold enough to go to where they are."

As I mentioned above, we are talking about actual physical resurrections, but the same principles apply in the spirit realm. Ministering life to the spiritually dead requires humility, the ability to hear God's voice, and the courage to obey when you hear it. We may have just a few opportunities to pray for the physically dead in our entire lifetimes, but we will have innumerable occasions to bring spiritual life to those who are spiritual corpses.

Chapter 3

How Not to Raise the Dead

Before we learn how to raise the dead, we ought to look at some of the ways people have tried to raise the dead unsuccessfully. There are several methods that we might feel inclined to try, but we will be wasting our time and leaving the corpses as dead as ever.

1. Make Them Feel Guilty for Dying

Obviously, we are talking about the spiritually dead at this point. It's pretty hard to make a corpse feel anything, including guilt, even though we might feel angry that someone we depended on died unexpectedly.

Whether through suicide, accident or sudden fatal illness, people can be taken from us when we least expect it, leaving us in shock and despair. If it was in our power, we certainly might have a strong desire to make them feel guilty. We might get angry and lose our cool; we might even throw a royal fit, but while it might relieve some of our pent up emotion, it will never bring them back.

But the same thing will hold true for those who are spiritually dead. We can not bring them back to life by making them feel guilty that they are dead. They don't even know that they are dead. They think they are just as alive as you are in most cases.

It may be your teenage or older child, who once sang all the songs in Sunday school and attended boys or girls clubs in your church. Today, they are living an ungodly life style and are spiritually dead in your estimation. What can you do to bring them back?

One of the normal tendencies is to verbally attack the person who has left the life of God and is living in spiritual death. Parents, whose own parents poured guilt on them with no positive results, tend to revert back to that failed strategy themselves.

But increasing the already heavy load of guilt drives the spiritually dead further away from the very people who should be the source of life for them. Guilt, condemnation and shame are all counter-productive when it comes to raising the spiritually dead.

How about nations or segments of society? How do you bring revival or resurrection life to a society that has forsaken God and turned to wickedness? Does it do any good to accuse people of being spiritually dead and evil? Can we bring them back to life by making them feel guilty for their awful sins?

Again, it is very counter-productive to accuse, get angry and condemn the wicked. If anything, most people only get worse and more evil when confronted by self-righteous Christians who are bent on telling them how wicked they are. We will deal with a better way in the coming chapters.

2. Dress Them Up to Look Alive

Embalmers are very gifted in making a corpse look like a living person. They replace the blood with embalming fluid and use everything at their disposal, including dress clothes and make-up to make them as alive and physically appealing as possible.

Spiritually dead people are often dressed up as well. They look like real living spiritual beings. They can speak Christianese, dress up in their Sunday best, and sing the hymns and choruses with everyone else on Sunday morning. How alive they can look, but they are not actually breathing, nor is the life-blood of Jesus flowing through their veins.

3. Give Them Some Medicine

Medicine is good if the person is still alive, but once they have died, medicine won't bring them back to life. In the same way, we can't revive a spiritually dead person with some spiritual pills. A little more church won't do the trick for someone who is spiritually dead. A little counseling or teaching is not going to bring them back to life. They need a miracle, not medicine. People can give medicine, but only God can produce that miracle.

4. Compare One Dead Corpse With Another

If we could look at several dead people at the same time, we might decide that one looked more alive than the others. But looking more alive than someone else that is also dead does not bring a corpse back to life. If you're dead, you're dead. The others are not deader, even if they look more dead. All the corpses are equally dead.

We must recognize that the same thing holds true for those who are spiritually dead. Comparing them to someone that is in worse shape than they are will not do them any good, any more than giving them medicine when it is already too late. Our only solution is to bring life to the corpse through the miracle power of Jesus.

Chapter 4

The Most Important Key to Raising the Dead

As we discussed in a previous chapter, there are a lot of things not required for raising the dead. We don't have to be recognized by man or religious institutions that might equip us with degrees or ordination papers or anything like that. We don't have to speak in King James English or even with perfect grammar in whatever language we may speak.

But there is one critical key—an indispensable necessity—to unlock the door to the kind of power that can raise a dead corpse and bring it back to life. Are you ready for this powerful revelation?

Here it is: **To bring dead people back to life you must be alive yourself.** I ask you, is this not a profound truth? That seems too simple doesn't it? But most profound truths are so simple that we can totally miss them.

Now the question is: Do you and I qualify? Are we alive? Do we have life flowing through us that we can give to others?

If someone has stopped breathing and you know how to do artificial respiration, you would open their mouth and breathe into their body. Obviously, you can only breathe into the other person's body the breath that you have first taken into your own body.

We have had first-hand experience with this natural form of breathing life into a body that has stopped breathing. Our daughter, Andrea, at the age of 16, stopped breathing after an asthma attack. While I drove as fast as I dared toward the hospital to meet the ambulance, Brenda was breathing into her stiffened-up body. She knew that Andrea was only getting a small percentage of the oxygen that she would get from breathing on her own, so she breathed a little harder than normal. That proved to be a good thing because, unknown to us, Andrea's lungs had actually collapsed, and at some point in the journey, she had experience a cardiac arrest.

At the same time, both of us were praying and warring with the prophetic words Andrea had received in the previous months and years. We don't know exactly how much difference the forced breathing made, but God did a miracle and began to bring Andrea back before she was completely gone. She had stopped breathing on her own for over ten or twelve minutes, but we saw signs of life in her body just before the medical team asked us to leave the room. Andrea totally recovered and has already fulfilled many of the words that had been prophesied over her.

Now please remember the game of life and death we shared earlier. If you were taken out by your enemy's elastic rubber ring, you were pronounced dead at the scene. But if someone who was still alive on your team came by and touched you, you could come back to life and join the battle again.

In both situations, it is required that you be one that is alive, before you can give life to others. Let's ask the question again: Are we ourselves alive? Do we have life to pass on to others? Can those dry bones that surround us in the open valley live again? I discovered a few Scriptural nuggets that I'd like to share with you related to this concept of transferring life.

Taking a Physical Examination

Imagine going to the doctor and taking a physical exam. At the conclusion of the physical, imagine how shocking it would be for him to report that according to the tests he had taken, you were actually already dead, but you just didn't know it yet. You would say, "But that's impossible, I know that I'm alive." Then he would tell you, "You seem to be alive, but your heart is not beating, you have completely stopped breathing, your liver and kidneys are not eliminating toxins and your brain has stopped functioning. I'm sorry to have to tell you this, but you are clinically dead."

While this may not ever happen in the doctor's office, it has happened in the spirit realm according to Scripture. Let's look at a few examples:

> *Then He said to me, "Son of Man, these bones are the whole house of Israel." (Ezekiel 37:31a)*

God was referring to the valley full of dry bones that He had commanded Ezekiel to bring back to life. These were living people, who would have assured you that they were very much alive. However, God saw them as not only dead, but as bones that were already very dry and disconnected from each other

> *I know your works, that you have a name that you are alive, but you are dead. (Revelation 3:1b)*

This was written to the Church in Sardis. They thought they were alive because of their religious activities, but Jesus saw them as dead. He exhorted them to strengthen what remained that was still alive, lest it should die as well.

> *These are clouds without water, carried about by the winds; late autumn trees without fruit, twice dead, pulled up by the roots. (Jude 12b)*

Jude was talking about people who had slipped into the church unawares and were causing many problems in the church. He called them "twice dead", perhaps meaning that they had been made alive to God after having been dead in sin, but had since forsaken His ways to seek their own personal advantage as part of the flock. They were now "dead" again.

But she who lives in pleasure is dead while she lives.
(I Timothy 5:6)

This verse is about widows and whether they should be supported by the church. His bold declaration is that although she may still be alive, a widow who lives in pleasure (obviously not the pleasures we enjoy at His right hand), is actually dead from God's viewpoint.

These and other Scriptures make it clear that we can think we are alive when God sees us as dead. While we are encouraged to die to our fleshly desires, we don't want to ever be found dead to God and to His Spirit.

Remember what a great beginning and anointing King Saul had to lead? He started out humble and true, but he forgot to stay humble and began to think he could function as priest, along with fulfilling his kingly duties. The result was that "The Spirit of the Lord departed from Saul" (I Samuel 16:14a). Instead, David was blessed with the anointing which Saul had carried. Saul, on the other hand was troubled by a "distressing spirit." Apparently, Saul was ignorant of the change, and he tried to function as if nothing had happened.

It is very interesting to note that the word for "breath" is the same as "spirit" in the Hebrew and the Greek. Ezekiel was told to call for the wind or breath to come into the dead corpses. The breath or Spirit of life can blow upon us, but, as Jesus said in John 3:8, the wind comes and goes without anyone actually seeing it come and go. Saul didn't see the Spirit of God coming and he never saw it leaving. That Spirit is the Spirit of Life, and without being full of that Spirit of Life, we will never be able to breathe life into any person who is dead, whether he is physically dead or spiritually dead.

So how do we know if we are spiritually dead or alive? That is a good and valid question, which is not designed to bring fear and doubt, but to bring the assurance and confidence that God can and will use you to raise the dead for His glory and honor.

Vital Signs That We Are Truly Alive

1. You have a pulse.

A pulse indicates your heart is beating and blood is flowing through your veins. Spiritual life is dependent on your spiritual heart. If your heart is beating with love for God and for the people He created to bring joy to His heart, you have spiritual life. John said that we know we have passed from death to life if we love His kids (author's paraphrase of I John 3:14).

Does God's love flow through you to those in need? Do you ever sacrifice your own comfort and well-being to help someone who is hurting, just because you feel the compassion of Jesus for them? Do you weep with those who weep when they suffer the loss of a loved one because Jesus weeps through you for them? If so, His life is in you and you are a candidate for raising the dead.

2. You are breathing.

Every living creature sustains life by continuing to breathe in the air that contains life-giving oxygen. The oxygen is distributed through the blood to every cell of the body. At the same time the cells give off their toxins, including carbon dioxide, to the same blood cells that brought them the oxygen. The blood carries the carbon dioxide and other toxins back to the lungs to be expelled as the lungs exhale. Breathing is a never-ending process through which the body is continually enriched and detoxified.

Do you breathe the Spirit of Life into your being and exhale the toxic waste that is constantly trying to poison your system? Many Christians feel that because they notice toxins in their walk with God that they are total failures and not usable by God. But our respiratory and cardio-vascular systems illustrate the error of that thinking. Our flesh is always trying to poison our spirit, but if we keep breathing the life of God into us, we will be constantly purifying our inner man, just as we purify the physical body.

Deep breathing is a practice we have been taught for health purposes. When you breathe deeper, you take in more oxygen and you get rid of more toxins which can lay low in your lungs. The same advice is appropriate for spiritual health. We need to breathe deeply of the Holy Spirit. Spiritual breathing involves taking in spiritual oxygen through Bible reading and meditation, soaking and constant communication. It also involves giving off the toxins through humble worship and confession of sin.

But exhaling or breathing out involves more than getting rid of toxins. Our breath also contains some unused oxygen and even the carbon dioxide is health-giving for plant life. When we breathe out spiritually, we are also giving praise and thanks to God. And when we breathe the breath of life into someone who has stopped breathing, they are receiving the extra oxygen that you have taken in and have not used up.

To sum up, we have two choices as Christians. We can be alive and sickly, or we can be alive and healthy.

A lot of it has to do with the way we breathe. Those who want to give life to others should breathe deeply in the presence of God and take in as much of His life as they possibly can. You can only give away what you have yourself.

3. You change and grow.

Everything alive is in a state of growth or at least change. Cells are constantly reproducing and multiplying. Bodies may stop growing taller, but the cells are still reproducing to replace dying ones and changes are taking place in the body. It is usually either growing in size or it is going through the aging process, which is still evidence that the body is alive. At any rate, when death finally comes, the cells of the body stop multiplying and decay sets in. That decay is an outside force, where living organisms now feed on that which is dead.

We know that we are spiritually alive if we are experiencing growth or change. When we stop changing, we have lost our life. Living beings move, work, play, communicate, interact, produce and change.

Signs of spiritual life include dissatisfaction with the status quo of your walk with God. A corresponding sign is a hunger and thirst for more of God. When your spiritual gifts are maturing you know you are alive. When you are reproducing your gifts in others and raising children to use their gifts, you know you are alive.

There are many other vital signs of life in a physical body that we could discuss, but these three should suffice to convince you that you are indeed alive spiritually. If for some reason this analysis leaves you with the impression that you are actually spiritually dead, there is good news. Jesus is ready and willing to breathe pure high octane spiritual life into your being.

You don't have to do anything other than admit to your need for His life in your spirit and ask Him to do it. He will do the rest. He will even make you a member of His own family according to John 1:11-12. Jesus breathed life into his disciples who had deserted Him in His hour of need. And He is very willing and ready to breathe everlasting life into your spirit, so that you too can breathe life into anyone who has died.

Chapter 5

Elijah and Elisha Raise the Dead

There are basically just two different ways that people were raised from the dead in Scripture. One way was simply speaking or prophesying to the dead person. The other way was to physically touch the body to transfer life from the body of the living to the body of the dead. Some resurrections involved both touching and prophesying to the body. Let's look at several cases from the Old Testament.

Elijah raises the widow's son.

Elijah had prophesied a drought in Israel, which lasted three and one half years. After having been fed by ravens, he was sent by God to Zaraphath in Sidon because the brook he had been drinking from had finally dried up. In Zaraphath he met a widow woman and her son who were about to make their final meal, because they had reached the very bottom of the barrels of flour and oil.

Elijah asked the widow to feed him first and promised her that she would not run out of food until the famine was over. God did the miracle and all of their lives were spared.

But even though their lives had been spared miraculously from starvation, the son got sick and finally died. The mother asked Elijah if he had come to bring punishment for her sin by killing her son. Elijah responded by simply asking her to give him the body of the child. Then he took the little corpse from her arms and carried him to his own bed in the upper room.

What he did next was something that would be repeated by others later, including the Apostle Paul. Elijah stretched out his body on the body of the boy and prayed with passion to God. Like the widow, he also questioned God's ways, asking:

> *O Lord my God, have you also brought tragedy on the widow with whom I lodge, by killing her son? (I Kings 17:20b)*

God was apparently not offended, but listened to the passionate prayer of Elijah. We read in I Kings 17:22:

> *Then the Lord heard the voice of Elijah; and the soul of the child came back to him, and he revived.*

What we are looking for when we raise the dead is for the soul (or spirit) to return to the body that it has already vacated. A body that has all of its physical parts intact is of little use without the soul or spirit living in it. In this example of raising the dead, Elijah did not speak to the child. He prayed to God and he put his body on top of the boy's body. This was a body-to-body transfer of life from the living to the dead. Elijah was filled with and had the power of life flowing through him, and that life could be transferred from his body to the body of a dead person.

Elijah did not just lay himself on the body, but he cried out to God for the miracle. As far as we know, there was no history of people being raised from the dead, and there is no biblical record of such an event until this story. It took a bold faith, along with compassion and desperation for Elijah to ask for this unprecedented miracle. But responding to his spiritual instincts, he did it and God heard and answered his prayer.

Elisha has a double-portion resurrection ministry.

Elisha received Elijah's mantel, but he wanted even more than what Elijah had. He asked for a double portion of Elijah's anointing and was given his request. Elisha was credited with having performed twice the number of miracles that Elijah had, and instead of raising just one person from the dead, he raised two.

Actually, when Elisha died, he was still one miracle short of having received his "double-portion" promise given through Elijah. But God hadn't forgotten, and after he was buried in a tomb, God used Elisha's bones to resurrect a dead soldier thrown into his grave; but more of that later. Let's look at the first resurrection that took place when Elisha was still alive. You'll find the story in detail in II Kings, chapter four.

Elisha's First Resurrection

Interestingly enough, the first resurrection that took place through Elisha's ministry had a lot of things in common with the resurrection that took place through Elijah. Both involved women who took care of the prophets. Elijah's hostess was a widow, while Elisha's was a "great woman" who had an older husband. The widow already had a son when Elijah came to stay with them, while the "great woman" Elisha stayed with had no son. The first miracle she received was the miraculous birth of a son, as opposed to the multiplication of food enjoyed by the widow woman. But similar to what happened in Elijah's ministry, the son got sick and died.

Another similarity is that both boys were laid on the prophet's bed. Elisha was not on the scene when the son died, so the mother took him and laid him on Elisha's bed, just as Elijah had laid the widow's son on his own bed. Perhaps Elisha's "great woman" hostess had heard the story of the resurrection of the widow's son and what Elijah had done. At any rate, she didn't put her son on his own bed or hers; she put him on the bed where the prophet slept. The she went out to find Elisha and to bring him to her son. Obviously, she hoped that what had happened with Elijah could also happen with Elisha.

When people hear of certain types of miracles taking place with others they know, it encourages their faith to believe for their own miracles. The same is true for the miracle of raising the dead. We don't have much faith for raising the dead because in our society we don't know of many people who have experienced it or seen it happen. But Elijah pressed through and broke the doubt barrier and demonstrated God's power to raise someone from the dead. There should be many Elisha's with a passion ready to follow and do twice the miracles that their Elijah has done

When the distraught mother finally reached Elisha, she fell at his feet and held on to them. Gehazi, Elisha's servant, tried to push her away, but Elisha gave this interesting response:

Let her alone; for her soul is in deep distress, and the Lord has hidden it from me, and has not told me. (II Kings 4:27b)

Elisha was moving in such an anointing that it was normal for him to know what was going on without being told. But in this case, he declared that the Lord had hidden this knowledge from him. Perhaps the Lord kept Elisha from knowing the boy's true condition and delayed his coming on the scene so that there would be no doubt that he was actually dead. By the time he got to where the boy was lying, the boy must have been dead for some time. It reminds me a little of the case of Lazarus, where Jesus delayed his trip to Bethany, and Lazarus was dead for four days before He was resurrected. It made the miracle that much more undeniable, as well as remarkable.

The boy's mother, still clutching the feet of Elisha, then made her complaint against him for giving her a son in the first place. Instantly, Elisha knew what was wrong. He sent his servant, Gehazi, with his staff and instructed him to lay the staff on the face of the child.

This is an interesting aspect of the story and builds upon the concept of the transfer of healing power through objects associated with the prophet. First we read that Elijah laid the dead child on his own bed. Then we read that the mother in this story laid her dead son on Elisha's bed. Now, Elisha tells his servant to lay his own staff on the child's face.

Neither being on the prophet's bed, nor laying the prophet's staff on the dead child's face brought either child back to life. However, it was obvious that both the prophets and the mother of this child believed that there was some potential benefit and power associated with objects that had been in extended physical contact with the prophets. We do have a good example of this in the New Testament, where we read:

Now God worked unusual miracles by the hands of Paul, so that even handkerchiefs or aprons were brought from his body to the sick and the diseases left them and the evil spirits went out of them. (Acts 19:11)

Luke, the writer of Acts, does not even say that Paul prayed for these pieces of cloth. It just says that they had touched his body. Clearly, as we will continue to see, there is something to this concept of the healing anointing and resurrection life being transferred from a physical human body to a non-human object and then to another physical human body. Somehow, in some way, the cloth carried the anointing and transferred it to another person. Certainly, Elijah and Elisha, as well as the mother of the child, believed in the concept of the transfer of anointing, or they would not have done what they did.

When Gehazi saw that nothing was happening, he returned to meet Elisha and told him that the child had not awakened. When Elisha finally arrived back at his little apartment, he found the child still lifeless—a completely dead corpse. The boy was not "just barely" dead. He was totally and completely dead. By this time it could not be contested that he was just unconscious.

Seeing the lifeless child, Elisha did something that

other men of faith did in various other parts of Scripture. He went in alone to the corpse, shutting the door behind him. Jesus did the same with the daughter of Jairus in Luke 8:54 and in Acts 9:40, Peter did the same thing with Dorcas. A common belief is that these leaders all wanted to control the spiritual atmosphere and keep out any spirit of doubt that might be in the crowd of observers. It could also have been a means of removing distractions while they communicated with God about the situation.

After closing the door, Elisha prayed to God and then stretched his body out on the body of the child. He was mouth to mouth, eyes to eyes and hand to hand, according to II Kings 4:34. The response was that the boy's body began to warm up. Then Elisha did some pacing and praying and returned to the boy, repeating the body-to-body contact again. This time the boy sneezed seven times and opened his eyes.

Elisha called his servant and told him to call the boy's mother. She once again fell at his feet and bowed to the ground, before she picked up her son and went out. Her intense anguish and desperation had turned into intense gratitude and appreciation.

Elisha's Second Resurrection

As we mentioned above, Elisha died with only one resurrection to his credit. He was also one short of having twice the miracles attributed to Elijah. But God was not finished with Elisha, even after he was dead. The most unusual resurrection of all occurred some time after he retired from active ministry on the earth. The Bible tells this brief story:

> *Then Elisha died, and they buried him. And the raiding bands from Moab invaded the land in the spring of the year. So it was, as they were burying a man, that suddenly they spied a band of raiders; and they put the man in the tomb of Elisha; and when the man was let down and touched the bones of Elisha, he revived and stood on his feet. (II Kings 13:20-21)*

One can only wonder how the Moabites reacted to the dead man standing on his feet, totally alive. But however they reacted, they must have taken note that they had seen something very unusual and that the man whose bones their buddy had contacted must have carried a powerful anointing.

It would be safe to say that Elisha's dead bones carried more life in them than many people who seem to be totally alive. We will look into that scenario in the next section as we check out the whole valley of dry bones that Ezekiel encountered in chapter thirty-seven of his prophetic book.

It seems appropriate that we should also comment on the apparent contradiction of our earlier proposition, namely, that one must be alive in order to transfer life to the dead. We said that dead men or women could not transfer life, but living men or women could.

Clearly, Elisha was dead, so how could life transfer through his dead bones? Obviously, God looks at things differently than we do. Elisha may have been physically dead, but his bones apparently had not lost the spiritual anointing of life that had flowed through him in better times. Meanwhile, of all the millions of God's people who were physically alive, there was not one record of any of them transferring life to a dead corpse. As we said, God sees things differently than man.

Let's sum up what we have learned so far. Elijah and Elisha were involved in a total of three resurrections. Common factors in the first two cases included prayer and the physical transfer of life from the living to the dead. Physical objects such as the prophet's bed and Elisha's staff were also used for the obvious purpose of transferring life from the body of the prophets to the dead children.

The final resurrection involved no technique or strategy, since Elisha was dead himself. There was however, an obvious transfer of life from the bones of Elisha to the corpse.

Thus, we can conclude that in all three of these Old Testament cases, people who carried a strong miracle anointing had the capacity to transfer life from their own bodies to the dead bodies which they encountered.

Chapter 6

Ezekiel Prophesies Life to Dry Bones

Although Ezekiel is not credited with any particular natural or physical resurrection, his experience in Ezekiel 37 with the valley of dry bones reveals tremendous insights for us as we learn more about the phenomenon of raising the dead. It gives us clear principles related to resurrection, both spiritually and physically.

You probably know the story. Ezekiel was carried in the Spirit and set down in the middle of a valley that was full of "very dry" bones. God spoke to him and asked him if the bones could live. When Ezekiel was non-committal, God told him to prophesy to the bones. After the bones came together and flesh and skin covered the bones, God spoke to him again and told him to prophesy to the breath or wind, which also means spirit, so that life would fill and empower each reassembled and reconstructed body.

Ezekiel reports:

So I prophesied as He commanded me, and breath came into them, and they lived, and stood upon their feet, an exceedingly great army. (Ezekiel 37:10)

God then explained the object lesson to Ezekiel. He said:

These bones are the whole house of Israel. (Ezekiel 37:11)

God had shown Ezekiel how He saw things differently than humans see them. With normal, natural eyes, we would see normal men, women and children. They would be doing the things that normal human beings do, and they would look very much alive to us.

However, God saw them as not only sickly, diseased, or dismembered, etc., but also as totally and completely dead and dried up. He was looking at the spirits of men and women, not their physical bodies. God then declared that the house of Israel, which was covered with a spirit of hopelessness, would be breathed upon by His Spirit, the Spirit of Life, and they would live and be placed back in their own land.

God Reveals a New Covenant Resurrection Principle

Both Elijah and Elisha raised the dead in similar

fashion. Two things were involved in their resurrection experiences:

1. They prayed to God.
2. They transferred life from their bodies (or their remains) to the dead bodies.

Ezekiel's spiritual experience gives us a preview of something new that believers would do to raise the dead in the New Testament. Ezekiel was not told to pray or to physically touch the dry bones. He was simply told to prophesy to them.

Prophesying or speaking life into something that is dead is a New Covenant resurrection principle that was never applied in the Old Testament accounts where the dead were raised.

When Ezekiel prophesied to the dead bones, he was told to address them and say:

Oh dry bones, hear the word of the Lord! Thus says the Lord God to these bones: "Surely I will cause breath to enter into you, and you shall live." (Ezekiel 37:4-5)

Ezekiel simply spoke the words that God gave him to say to the lifeless bones. Of course, this makes no sense. It makes more sense to pray to God to do the miracle. Why speak to dead objects? But this is precisely what we find Jesus and His apostles doing in several of the New Testament resurrection accounts.

The power of the prophetic word should not be underestimated in the realm of the supernatural. As I discovered in my research for a previous book entitled *Prophetic Ministry: Strategic Key to the Harvest,* prophetic ministry is the normal precursor to a release of the miraculous power of God.

Of course, prophecy depends on listening to God and hearing His voice. We can't just say whatever we want, whenever we want.

"If any man speaks, let him speak as the oracle of God." (I Peter 4:11)

Those who have actually been used to raise the dead must ultimately submit to the plan and will of God. Supresa Sithole (*Surprise* in English), International Director of Iris Ministries, the ministry of Rolland and Heidi Baker, has been involved in at least three resurrections. He shared with me that they have prayed for others to be raised, but sometimes God made it clear that His plan was not to bring the dead person back. In one case, he was given a vision of the hearse taking the body away and had to tell the family members that the dead person would not be revived.

There are some exceptions to this principle, however. Sometimes, God allows His plans to be altered by those who appeal to His mercy and grace. One example is Hezekiah, who was told to get his house in order, because he was going to die. When he wept before the Lord, God had mercy and added fifteen years to his life. Moses also was used to intercede for the Israelites, when God threatened to wipe them off the face of the earth. God modified His judgments in response to Moses' intercession.

A more recent story, which makes it clear that God sometimes allows His servants to influence His decisions, comes from the life of Smith Wigglesworth. When his wife died, Smith took the authority over death that he had wielded very successfully on many occasions (one of his former associates claimed that there were over ninety resurrections in his ministry). He boldly commanded her spirit to return to her body. God responded to His anointed servant and she revived. However, as I remember the story, she sat up and said to him, "Smith Wigglesworth, what are you doing? Let me go." He then gave in and let her return to Heaven.

The Breath of Life

Because of a very busy schedule, I had to take time out from writing this portion of the chapter. God had planned the timing so that I would not waste time writing something that would have to be redone later. The reason was that He had more revelation to reveal to me on this subject, which took place in the past few days.

I owe some of the revelation that I am about to share to my good friend and fellow-author, Jeff Doles, of Walking Barefoot Ministries. I was given the opportunity to read and endorse the manuscript of his book, *God's Word in Your Mouth*. The insights revealed were very pertinent to this book, and I know that these new insights will greatly enhance its message.

We Were Created in His Image to Do What He Does

Jesus told His disciples, "As the Father has sent Me, I also send you." (John 20:21b). I never thought of the fact that Jesus was revealing the pattern that the Godhead had established way back in the days of creation. When God created the heavens and the earth, He created man, "in His image and after His likeness." He created someone not only just like Him in many ways, but He was creating beings that would continue to do what He had been doing.

As Jesus trained His disciples to expand His Kingdom by doing what He had done, so God created men and women to expand or "fill and subdue" the earth by doing what He had just finished doing. What had God been doing?

1. He had been speaking creatively.
2. He had been breathing life into man.

So what does God want us to do? I believe He wants us to speak creatively and to breathe life into men.

Breath, Speech and Life are Closely Related

Without breathing you can't live and you can't speak. But if you can breathe, you are probably alive and you can most likely speak. Breath, wind and spirit are translated in the New Testament from the same Greek word—*pneuma*. Try putting that in John 3:5-8. Without adding the grammatical endings of the Greek, it would read like this:

> *Jesus answered, "Most assuredly, I say to you, unless one is born of water and the Pneuma, he cannot enter the Kingdom of God.*

> *"Do not marvel that I said to you, 'You must be born again.'*

> *"That which is born of the flesh is flesh and that which is born of the Pneuma is pneuma.*

> *"The pneuma blows where it wishes, and you hear the sound of it, but cannot tell where it comes from*

and where it goes. So is everyone who is born of the Pneuma."

Breath, wind and spirit are so similar in nature that the Greek language uses the same word for each one. Understanding this helps us understand our purpose for being on the earth.

God breathed on His first disciples—Adam and Eve.

Jesus breathed on His eleven disciples after His resurrection.

The Holy Spirit of God breathed on Jesus, and He come back to life through Divine resuscitation. Jesus was now breathing Resurrection Life and able to transfer that Resurrection Life to His disciples.

I believe Jesus was giving us a great example. As soon as He had declared that He was sending them like His Father had sent Him, He breathed on them and said, "Receive the Holy Pneuma." It had never occurred to me that He might be saying that He wanted us to breathe on others the way He had breathed on His own disciples. In the next verse, Jesus declares that they have the power of life and death in them, saying,

> *"If you forgive the sins of any, they are forgiven them; if you retain the sins of any, they are retained." (John 20:23)*

Although I don't totally understand the meaning of

this verse, it is clear that God is revealing the fact that He is imparting incredible authority to His disciples as His representatives or ambassadors on the earth. The disciples were to become the foundations of the church, which is His very own body. In other words, they would replace His physical body on the earth and do what He would have done if He were still walking the streets of Jerusalem, the hills of Judea and the shores of Galilee.

This tremendous power and authority would come upon them at Pentecost, but they had already had the first taste of it when Jesus breathed upon them. Like faith itself, which is the substance and evidence or down payment of what is to come, the Pneuma that came from Jesus' mouth, was the prelude or appetizer for the mighty rushing Pneuma that would come down from Heaven, accompanied by the fire of the Holy Pneuma.

As Jeff Doles relates in *God's Word in Your Mouth*, Adam's mandate was to speak to the animals and give them their identity. Names are important to God and describe the nature or character of their owners. Adam was given the authority to do what God had been doing, although it would not be on the same level. God had spoken and created the earth and its creatures. Adam was speaking and creating in each creature an awareness of their purpose and function by giving them names.

In Ezekiel 37, the prophet is told to speak or prophesy to the dry bones and assign a new name to them.

They had been previously named, "Hopeless Dry Bones." Ezekiel spoke and prophesied a new name to them, which was "Mighty Army of the Lord." God is calling us to give new names to the "Hopeless Dry Bones" in our world.

Those who have been named "Weak," we will rename "Strong in the Lord." Those named "Poor," we will rename "Rich in Jesus." Those named "Badly Defeated," we will rename "More than Conqueror." Those named "Total Failure," we will rename "Successful Saint." Wherever we go, we will take seriously Adam's commission to assign names to those who have not received their names from God, and we will give them an awareness of their destiny and purpose for being created.

We will do this through the anointed words that God says are already in our mouths. See Deuteronomy 30:14, Isaiah 51:6, 59:21, and Romans 10:8. There are many other times that the Bible refers to the word of God in our mouths. Let us believe that He means what He says and that we can all prophesy life to dry bones. We are the children of Adam, who named the creations of God. We are the seed of Abraham, who believed what God said, even though it seemed impossible. We are the disciples of Jesus, who told us to do the works that He had done and even greater. We are children of the Father, who loves all of His children and made them in His image and after His likeness.

We have the inheritance, the birthright and the immediate presence of the Holy Pneuma—the breath of God in our mouths. We have a mandate to breathe and speak the words of life into whatever we see that is dead, as we are led by the Holy Pneuma of God. It's not enough to just be a "good example." If we are not speaking creative words of life; if our mouth is not saying the words that God put there; we are NOT being a good example. Jesus didn't just think His words—He spoke them.

Jesus spoke forgiveness to the woman taken in adultery and to the crippled man let down from the roof. He spoke faith to the man at the Pool of Bethesda when He told him to take up his bed and walk. Peter spoke hope to the cripple at the temple gate when he said, "Look at us ... silver and gold I do not have, but what I do have, I give you" (Acts 3:4, 6).

If we want to raise the dead—natural or spiritual—we must speak out the words that God has put in our mouth.

Prophesy to the Pneuma

The Old Testament was written in Hebrew, not Greek, so the word Pneuma is of course not the word used in Ezekiel. But, as in Greek, the same word is used for wind, breath and spirit. The King James Version says:

Prophesy unto the wind (ruach), son of man, and say to the wind (ruach), "Thus saith the Lord God, Come from the four winds (ruach) O breath (ruach) and breathe (naphach) upon these slain that they may live." (Ezekiel 37:9)

"Ruach," a noun, means wind, breath and spirit, as we have already stated.

"Naphach" is a verb which means "puff, inflate, blow and breathe."

The exciting truth revealed here is that we can prophesy to the Holy Spirit (Ruach) to come and puff on, or inflate, the dead corpses that we meet in this life. It is the Holy Ruach within us inspiring us to prophesy to the Holy Ruach of God to come to breathe (Naphach) on those who do not have the breath of life (Ruach) flowing through them. Then He lets us breathe Himself onto others.

As we go to the New Testament resurrections, we will see that people were raised from the dead in one of the two ways we have already discovered. Either there was living body to dead body contact, or there were prophetic proclamations that went forth out of the mouths of those who knew their authority over death and its power.

Chapter 7

Jesus Raises Many in Life and Death

The gospels record the stories of three individuals raised from the dead through the earthly ministry of Jesus. We are also told that there were many resurrections that happened at the time of his death on the cross. Finally, He Himself was raised from the dead, after which He breathed resurrection life into His eleven disciples.

Jesus had declared Himself to be the "Resurrection and the Life" when He came to raise Lazarus from the dead, and of course, Jesus has given us the calling to do what He did and to be His body on the earth. In a very real sense, as His body, we also are resurrection and life to those we meet who are less than totally alive.

Jesus Raises a Widow's Son in Nain (Just Southeast of Nazareth)

The first recorded resurrection in the Old Testament was a widow's son. The first resurrection preformed by Jesus was also a widow's son. I think God cares a lot about widow's and orphans. In Luke 7:13 we are told that when Jesus saw the woman (not the dead son), He had compassion on her. There was no reason to have compassion on the son. It was the mother who was suffering.

This particular miracle was not recorded in any of the gospels except Luke, who happened to be a medical doctor. This same doctor also traveled with Paul and his team and wrote the book of Acts, which is full of miracles, including at least two resurrections. It's always good to have a doctor around to document the facts when a miracle occurs.

Let's take a quick look at what Jesus did when He raised the widow's son back to life. Luke tells us that after Jesus looked on her and had compassion, He said to her, "Do not weep." Obviously, Jesus was stimulating her faith. Unless He planned on doing something about the death, it would be cruel to tell a grieving widow not to weep.

Then Jesus came and touched the open coffin. It does not say that He touched the body, just the coffin. Then those who carried the coffin stood still, obviously wandering what He was going to do.

Finally, Jesus spoke directly to the corpse saying, "Young man, I say to you, arise." The young man sat up and began to speak, and Jesus presented him to his mother. Again, Luke makes it clear that the miracle was for her. By speaking to him, Jesus was breathing upon him. Remember breath, air and spirit are the same word in both Greek and Hebrew, and speaking requires breath passing through the mouth. Jesus was giving the young man a prophetic command, and speaking life into his dead body. The widow's son responded by obeying the command and speaking himself. I would have liked to have been there to hear what he talked about.

My guess is that he would have been talking about what he had seen in the spirit realm. He may have even been disappointed to have been brought back to life, but I also expect that he totally recognized who Jesus was, having been in the realm of the spirit. He may have been informing all around him that Jesus was the Messiah. At any rate, the breath of life came with creative power, and the young man was responding with words of life to create faith in others.

We do know that the people responded to the miracle, saying,

"A great prophet has risen up among us"; and, "God has visited His people" (Luke 7:16).

This first resurrection of Jesus was not in the pattern of Elijah and Elisha, which involved the physical body-to-body transfer of life, but in the pattern of Ezekiel's experience in Ezekiel 37, which involved the breath of life using the spoken word of prophecy.

Jesus Raises Jairus' Daughter

The second recorded resurrection in Luke is found just a chapter later in Luke 8. Jairus was a ruler of the synagogue and in desperation he fell at Jesus' feet and begged Him to come and heal His twelve year old daughter who was dying. Jesus said He would come and began to follow Jairus to his house.

The healing mission took an unexpected turn when Jesus was interrupted by a sudden flow of power leaving His body. He turned to ask who had touched Him. Of course, many had touched Him in the crowd, but finally a woman, who had suffered for twelve years with a flow of blood, acknowledged that she had touched His garment, believing that she would be healed. Jesus released her to enjoy her healing saying that her faith had made her well.

Before Jesus had finished His words to this happy lady, a messenger from the house of Jairus arrived and suggested that he let Jesus go His way because his daughter had already died. Jesus quickly spoke words of comfort and encouragement to Jairus, telling him to believe and not be afraid because his daughter would still be made well.

This is a beautiful example of the creative power of words that are breathed from the mouth of one who has the Holy Pneuma living and moving in Him. Jesus, as we know, was constantly listening to His Father, through the voice of the Holy Pneuma. He was speaking what He knew the Father desired, and He was speaking and creating faith in the mind and heart of Jairus.

Peter and John ministered in a similar way to the lame man at the temple in Acts 3. They spoke words that would build the faith of the lame man, according to the knowledge they had from the Holy Pneuma that it was his time to be healed. When we are allowing the Holy Pneuma to move and flow through our lives, as those who are spiritually alive and breathing, we will find it normal to prophesy words of faith, hope and love to those we encounter.

With that encouragement, Jairus brought Jesus to his house where the mourners had already gathered. Jesus exhorted them not to weep when He arrived and said that the little girl was not dead but only sleeping. Hearing this, the mourners and lamenters quickly transitioned into sarcastic mockers, not understanding His remarks or receiving His encouraging words. Those words could have been received to build their faith, but they did not know that they were dead dry bones, and they rejected Jesus' words of life.

Jesus then did something that we mentioned earlier when discussing Elijah and Elisha. He removed all the mourners from the house and allowed only Peter, James, John and the parents of the girl to stay. Obviously, Jesus wanted a little privacy for this resurrection. Many have commented on His reasons for this, but I don't think He was worried that His faith would waiver just because the mourners were filled with unbelief. We saw in the previous case that He didn't get rid of the crowd to raise the widow's son to life, but this case was more like those of Elijah and Elisha. Both Old Testament prophets raised their dead in private, behind closed doors.

Luke gives us the following details of the resurrection:

But He put them all outside, took her by the hand and called, saying, "Little girl, arise." Then her spirit returned, and she arose immediately. And He commanded that she be given something to eat. (Luke 8:54-55)

In the previous resurrection, Jesus only touched the coffin of the young man. In this one He took the little girl's hand as He spoke to her. Of the three recorded resurrections that Jesus performed, this is the only one where we find Him actually touching the body. We could speculate on the significance of this action, but whether He was transferring life through His anointed hand or just preparing to help her stand on her feet, what we do know is that He once again spoke to the person that was no longer in the body. He told her to arise and her spirit returned to her. Jesus was speaking to her pneuma and calling it back to her body that it might have life again.

When Jesus raised the widow's son, He also told him to arise. He was talking to the pneuma of the man like He was talking to the pneuma of the little girl. Jesus said in John 3 that when we are born of the pneuma, we are pneuma. We are not bodies that possess a spirit. We are spirits that are clothed in a body. God is Spirit (Pneuma), and those who worship Him must worship Him in spirit (pneuma) and in truth.

When Jesus raised the dead, He spoke as led by the Holy Pneuma to the pneuma of the person. As the Creator of every human pneuma, He had absolute and ultimate authority to command every human pneuma to come or go at His bidding. As those with His delegated authority, filled and controlled by the Holy Pneuma, we have the same power, as long as we, ourselves, are listening to the voice or breath of the Holy Pneuma.

Luke then tells us that "her spirit (pneuma) returned, and she arose immediately." When we raise the dead, we are looking for the spirit to return to the body. When the spirit returns to the body, the body is alive and able to arise.

Jesus then showed His concern for her physical being, telling her parents to give her some food. Her body needed nourishment after being sick for some time. She was completely whole physically, and her body was ready to function normally.

Lazarus Responds to the Voice of Jesus

The story of the resurrection of Lazarus takes up a full 44 verses in John 11. Much of the chapter deals with discussions between Jesus and His disciples and also between Jesus, Mary and Martha.

Jesus clearly is making a statement with this amazing miracle. It would not be very long until He would be in the tomb instead of Lazarus. He wanted His disciples to remember this resurrection to give them faith that He, Himself, would be resurrected as He was prophesying.

He intentionally delayed coming to Bethany when He heard that Lazarus was sick. He declared to Mary and Martha that because He is the Resurrection and the Life, their brother would rise again.

Jesus also taught them that if they believed in Him, they would never really die and they would see the glory of God. In their time of emotional upheaval, their understanding of His words was limited, but they were trying to grasp what He was saying. Jesus then released and revealed His emotions when He wept on the way to the tomb. Those who observed Him in Bethany interpreted his weeping as a sign that He loved Lazarus and was sad that He was gone.

My personal explanation for the weeping was that Jesus was thinking about how hard it was going to be for His friends and disciples when He was taken from them. They were so unbelieving when He was still with them. How would they make it when He was gone? He also knew what awaited Him, and Lazarus' death and the sorrow surrounding the whole scene would be multiplied when He would be taken, scourged and crucified.

Finally, when Jesus arrived at the tomb of Lazarus, which was a cave with a stone at the entrance, he ordered that the stone be removed. Again, I believe Jesus was making a statement to everyone who witnessed this event. Very soon, His body would be in a cave with a stone rolled in front of it. His Father in Heaven would send His angels to roll away that stone, just like He was telling others to roll the stone away from the grave of Lazarus.

Martha, who represents works without intimacy, protested that there would be a stench of decaying flesh after four days of burial. Jesus gently reminded her to believe and she would see the glory of God.

When the stone was rolled away, Jesus took the time to talk to His Father and thanked Him for hearing Him, and He declared that He just wanted to build faith in those standing by, knowing that His Father always heard Him. John then shares this brief account of the actual resurrection:

Now when He had said these things, He cried with a loud voice, "Lazarus, come forth!" And he who had died came out bound hand and foot with grave clothes, and his face was wrapped with a cloth. Jesus said to them, "Loose him, and let him go." (John 11:43-44)

The phrase, "Lazarus, come forth!" is surely one of the most remembered phrases in Scripture. Jesus didn't whisper these words or speak them behind closed doors in a house to a child on a bed. He obviously wanted everyone to hear and to know that He had the authority and power to bring life back to something that was totally and indisputably dead. Jesus cried out these words with emotion and strength because He knew that this one miracle would cause many to believe in Him, and it would also help His followers to believe in His own resurrection, in spite of the incredible horror of His coming death at Calvary.

Immediately, the spirit (pneuma) of Lazarus returned to His body and he obeyed the command of Jesus. Although wrapped completely in grave clothes, he was able to walk out of the cave and was released from the wrappings that spoke of death and bondage.

Lazarus quickly became an evangelist, leading many amazed Jews to believe in Jesus. He was so effective that the chief priests even plotted to put him to death along with Jesus.

Comparing Three Resurrections

Let's summarize briefly what we have observed in these three resurrections performed by Jesus.

In each of the three resurrections, Jesus spoke directly to the spirit of the person who had died. In each case,

He commanded them to do something, either to arise or come forth out of the grave.

In only one case did Jesus physically touch the body; when He took the hand of Jairus' little girl. Jesus depended almost completely on His authority and power to speak the word and have it obeyed. As New Testament disciples of Jesus, we should be walking in His footsteps and doing His works with His methods. His basic method, of course, was to listen to His Father and do what He said to do. In like manner, we can listen to the Holy Spirit and do what He says to do.

Graves Open When Jesus Dies

Mathew records the following account:

And Jesus cried out again with a loud voice, and yielded up His Spirit. Then, behold, the veil of the temple was torn in two from top to bottom; and the earth quaked, and the rocks were split, and the graves were opened; and many bodies of the saints who had fallen asleep were raised; and coming out of the graves after His resurrection, they went into the holy city and appeared to many. (Matthew 27:50-53)

Jesus, like Samson, accomplished more in His death than in His life. Not only did Jesus shed His blood to pay the penalty for our sins, which enabled us to be reconciled to God, but many more people were raised from the dead when He died than when He was alive.

When Jesus, whose voice created the universe, cried out, "It is finished" and "yielded up His Spirit," I believe something radical happened in the spiritual realm. We are told He descended into Hades to lead captivity captive (Ephesians 4:8-10). It's hard to imagine what kind of spiritual wind (pneuma) storms were created when that happened. Compared to a category four hurricane like Katrina, it was probably a category 500.

It's no wonder that the earth quaked, the temple veil was torn in two and graves were opened. Hades was in terror, being visited by the Judge and Master of every being in existence. The spirits of the righteous responded to that last great cry of Jesus on the cross. They obeyed the voice of their Master and returned to their original bodies just as Lazarus and the other two had done during Jesus' ministry on earth.

When Jesus said, "It is finished," He was saying that He had conquered death by dying and that Resurrection Life was now being released to all who would believe in Him. Jesus would return to His disciples after His resurrection and breathe that breath of life into them so that they might have the power to breathe the same breath of life into others and raise the dead.

There are many other great points in the passage

quoted above, but let me just focus on one thought as we close this chapter. This was Jesus' darkest hour, but it was also His finest hour. He had resisted the temptation to come down from the cross and vindicate Himself to all His tormentors. He had been faithful and true to the will of God in all His suffering, and now He could release a powerful explosion of the wind or breath (pneuma) of the Holy Spirit on His disciples. He would wait fifty days for the main event, but in the meantime, He would give a foretaste to those present of the kind of spiritual power which would be released.

The obvious application in our own lives is that when we seem to be in our darkest hour, and we feel like we are dying a painful death, then it's time to be aware of the power of God that can be released through us during such a dark hour. Resurrection life can only happen to us when we have been through a death experience. The more we let God "kill" our flesh, the more resurrection power we will have to raise others from the dead.

Since we are studying how to raise the dead, the above point is a valuable truth for all of us. When we fulfill the purpose and plan of God, without the praise and affirmation of men, and even at times become like a lamb going to the slaughter like Jesus did, without defending ourselves and fighting back, God can release into us what He released into Jesus. His power is for those who have been emptied of their own self-reliance and self-confidence. It is for those who have no back-up plan or security net. They are totally dependent and confident in the power and love of their God.

Chapter 8

Peter and Paul Minister Resurrection Life

The book of Acts contains two stories of the dead being raised by apostles. The apostles were named "apostles" because they were "sent out" by Jesus, even as the Father had sent Him to do His work. Thus, we should be able to see Jesus' methods repeated by His apostles. Let's take a look.

Peter Raises Dorcas

As the church spread throughout the countryside, Peter journeyed from place to place encouraging the saints. While he was in Lydda, a greatly loved and admired lady named Tabitha, or Dorcas, who lived in the city of Joppa, got sick and died. The saints in Joppa had heard that Peter was in nearby Lydda and sent word for him to come to Joppa.

When Peter arrived, the widows were weeping and showing him the garments that Dorcas had made for them. Luke describes how Peter handled the situation.

But Peter put them all out, and knelt down and prayed. And turning to the body, he said, "Tabitha, arise." And she opened her eyes and when she saw Peter she sat up. Then he gave her his hand and lifted her up; and when he had called the saints and widows, he presented her alive. (Acts 9:40-41)

Peter, like Elijah, Elisha and Jesus in certain situations, chose privacy over trying to raise the dead in public. I would guess that he just didn't want any distractions. He wanted to clearly hear God's voice in a situation like this.

We also read that Peter knelt down and prayed. We don't know what he said when he prayed, but he may have prayed something like Jesus prayed before He called Lazarus out of the tomb. He may have been thanking God for His miracle power and for hearing him, and/or he may have been asking God for the anointing needed for raising the dead.

I think it's good to point out that up until this time the only ones who had raised the dead were Elijah, Elisha and Jesus. This would be a first for Peter, although he had been used for many other miracles by this time, including the healing of hundreds, or perhaps thousands, as his shadow passed them on the street. This story is told in Acts 5:15-16, right after the sudden demise of Ananias and Sapphira.

Peter been used to perform just about every kind of miracle except raising the dead; but now that time had arrived. I think that I would also take a moment or two to talk to God before I talked to the dead body, if I was in Peter's shoes.

Then Peter turned to the body of Dorcas and commanded her to arise, following pretty much the pattern that Jesus set for him when He had raised the dead. The spirit (pneuma) of Dorcas heard the voice of Peter and recognized the authority of the Holy Spirit (Pneuma) speaking through Peter. The spirit of Dorcas came swiftly back to her body and she opened her eyes and sat up. Peter reached out his hand and lifted her to her feet. He then called the saints to the room and presented her to them alive.

This is a beautiful picture of what God wants to do with us when we minister to those who are spiritually dead. We can pray for wisdom and faith, and then we can prophesy to the Spirit of Life to come and inhabit them. When the Spirit of Life inhabits them, they will show true signs of life. However, we should still extend our hands to help them stand upright and prepare to serve the Lord. Sometimes we tend to step back and wait to see if they are going to make it or not in this spiritual walk of life. But they might need the helping hand of the one who breathed or spoke the breath of life into them.

When we have offered our hand to help them stand up, we can also invite those who have prayed for them and present them alive, allowing them to share their testimonies of God's amazing grace and power to resurrect what was dead. May God reveal to us the many opportunities He provides for us to raise the spiritually dead all around us.

Paul Raises a Sleeping Saint

On his way to Jerusalem, where he would be arrested, Paul visited the saints in Troas. Knowing that he had to leave the next day, and obviously full of things he wanted to share with them, Paul kept speaking until past midnight. A young man, named Eutychus, was sitting in an open window on the third floor and began to sink into a deep sleep. Luke then tells us:

> *As Paul continued speaking, he fell down from the third story and was taken up dead. But Paul went down, fell on him, and embracing him said, "Do not trouble yourselves, for his life is in him." Now, when he had come up, had broken bread, and eaten, and talked a long while, even till daybreak, he departed.*

And they brought the young man in alive, and they
were not a little comforted. (Acts 20:9-12)

This final New Testament account of an individual being raised from the dead provides us with some interesting information. This is the first case of the person involved in the cause of death also being the one involved in his resurrection. Paul's long-winded message finally put Eutychus to sleep, which in turn resulted in his death.

Paul also was the only person in the New Testament to use the body-to-body contact means of transferring life from the living to the dead. In addition, we have no record that Paul prayed to God or said anything to the deceased. We read only that while still embracing the young man, Paul spoke to the people who were there not to be troubled because his life was in him. In this case, Paul was prophesying to the people present and ministering the life of faith into their spirits.

I believe Paul was ministering spirit to spirit to Eutychus and calling his spirit back to him, possibly without speaking out loud for others to hear. At any rate, he clearly felt led to do what Elijah and Elisha had done and place his warm body over the body of the dead person.

Let's apply this lesson to the spiritually dead as well. There are people who need the warmth of our personal contact. They will not respond to just words, but they need us to embrace them with genuine love and concern. They are looking for an example of love and we won't have to say a lot. The anointing that is on us can fall on them when we get close to them, in a similar way that people were healed when Peter's shadow passed over them.

Sometimes we also need to speak words of encouragement to the relatives of the dead person and let our actions do the talking with the person who needs a resurrection. This could especially apply to young men and women who are the "living dead," in bondage to sin, without purpose and without hope. The relatives may trouble themselves with fear and vain efforts to convert them, but they may need someone like my friend, Sara Trollinger, the founder and President of House of Hope Ministries. Sara embraces many young people who have being given up for dead by others. She has seen hundreds of them turn their lives around and express the beautiful life of Jesus to all who meet them.

Heidi Baker is another example of a "hugger" who sees both natural and spiritual miracles as she hugs the "one" in front of her. Blind eyes and deaf ears are being opened (again, both in the natural and the spiritual). From the youngest AIDS baby to the elderly grandmas, she transfers the life of Jesus into their spirits and their bodies.

It's not too surprising that at this writing, Iris Ministries has documented around sixty physical resurrections in the past few years. We will share more details in the next chapter.

Chapter 9

Modern Day Resurrections

Physical Resurrections

The first person who shared his resurrection experience with me and our little congregation was a red-headed pastor, whose name I have forgotten. This was at least 20 years ago in Raymond, Washington. I do remember that he was with his wife in a remote place, and it seems to me it was in Alaska. At any rate, he died with no one around but his wife. She refused to give up praying for him and after about thirty minutes he began to breathe again and was completely restored. Of course, I can't prove his story to be true, but his story did remind me that God still wants us to raise the dead.

Another story was told to us by a prophet named Timothy Sherman, a man who helped us to activate our own prophetic ministry. He arrived at an accident scene where someone had just died. God told him to call the person back to life. Again, I don't remember many details, but I know that the dead person came back to life.

Indian Baby Revived

I do have one story with at least some of the important details, as written for me by the person that Jesus used to raise the dead child. Her name is Ruth Allison, and she is a beautiful senior citizen who could be retired, but goes to the mission field frequently. She recently spent six months in India helping to launch a Father's House home for orphans. Ruth is a very humble lady and a faithful intercessor, who has been serving the Lord in a beautiful way. I had heard from others about the child that been raised from the dead, and I asked her to write me her story, which she was willing to do.

This story took place in June of 2005 in Madras State of southeast India. The following is her story:

I was living in an apartment above a little Christian church, WAY out in the country! The Pastor and his wife were gone, when a loud banging began on my window about 8:00 p.m. A couple had brought, by bus, their 18-month-old daughter, who was severely dehydrated. They were desperate and wanted the pastor to pray for her. As he was gone, a woman who lived nearby, who spoke a few words of English, came to get me.

I went downstairs and prayed for the baby, who had been vomiting and with diarrhea for 5 days. This was the night of the 6th day, and she had had nothing to eat (or drink) for over 24 hours, and was semi-conscious.

I prayed for an hour—at that point her eyes rolled up in her head, and her head began lolling. She was really unconscious. The parents began screaming in Tamil that their baby had gone blind. They would not quiet down, but I kept on praying.

About 10:00, Sanji took a big breath in, breathed out—and then would not breathe in again. Her head fell back over my arm. I picked up her arm and dropped it; it was dead weight (no pun intended!). I was sitting cross-legged on a concrete floor in the middle of an empty church, holding a dead baby.

To this day I do not know how I stood up still holding the little girl, but I did. I was desperate!! For about 10 seconds I panicked (I thought they might kill me), but the Holy Spirit immediately brought the promises of God to my mind. I began to walk the floor, reminding God about how these people (who also practiced some Hinduism along with their Christianity) were depending upon Jesus, how it would glorify His name, and how He could not abandon those who called upon Him ... I prayed every promise I could think of, but I did not prophesy life over Sanji. After 6 or 7 of the world's longest minutes, she took a deep breath and began to breathe again. I continued to pray, and about 11:00 I felt the Lord release me, saying it was accomplished. Sanji's eyes again came down and she fluttered her fingers and turned away when I tried to offer her some water. She would not nurse or move, but I knew God had healed her; she was asleep after the ordeal.

At midnight—after 4 hours of prayer—I gave her back to her mother, telling her that Jesus said she was alright, and I went upstairs to bed. The parents did not think she would be OK, because after this long ordeal she still did not look good.

At 2:00 a.m., there was again a loud hoo-ha and banging on my window. Amalu (the Indian woman who spoke some English), was screaming that it was a miracle! A miracle!!! Sanji was awake and nursing. She did not throw up, and did not develop diarrhea again—she was hungry, energetic, and completely healed. The parents went home early in the morning when the buses started running.

More Resurrections in India

I'd like to quote now from the book "Megashift" in which Jim Rutz records the following stories on pages 3 and 4:

At six o'clock on an April evening in 2001, five-year-old Arjun Janki Dass died in New Delhi from an accidental electrocution.

His parents took him to a medical clinic where they worked on his body for two hours—without success. The doctor charged them 5,000 rupees (about $110) and told them to call a mortician.

Instead they called Rodrick at the nearby Deliverance Church. He then called upon Savitri, one of his staff members.

Savitri brought two other Christians to Arjun's home and the five of them began praying over the dead body about 10:00 p.m. They prayed their hearts out for six hours. Then at 4:00 a.m. the next morning, Arjun snapped back to life—no brain damage, no problems.

Today, he's a normal eight-year old kid. I met with Savitri, Arjun, and his mother, Mina (photos in center of book—page 137), and the boy is A-OK, except for a nasty scar behind his left ear where the wire hit.

Savitri is a 60-year-old widow, a Dalit ("untouchable") from the lowly Dom caste. She spent her life as a street sweeper, which made her, in the caste system, the lowest of the low. The broom was her livelihood, and she remains today a fine, humble lady, a former Hindu turned to Christ.

As we were parting, I asked Savitri through an interpreter, "How many resurrections have you been involved with in the six years that you've been doing ministry?"

She answered quietly, "Sixteen."

For a moment, my brain froze. Then I began to re-evaluate my life.

I would give you Savitri's e-mail address so you could check her out for yourself, but she doesn't have one. She can't read.

Jim Rutz also records the highly documented resurrection of a pastor in Onitsha, Nigeria. German evangelist

Reinhard Bonnke was speaking in a large church. The pastor had crashed his car the morning of Friday, November 30, 2001, and died being transported to a hospital. By 11:30 p.m. that night, two doctors had confirmed his death. Pastor Daniel Ekechukwu's body was taken to the morgue, and his body was prepared for embalming, receiving injections of chemical preservatives.

Two days after the accident and death, Daniel's wife, filled with faith for a miraculous resurrection, insisted on taking her husband's corpse to the church where Bonnke was speaking. The security people did not want to let her in, but she was allowed to take her husband's "stiff-as-an-iron-rod" body into the basement, which was the children's department. Bonnke never knew what was happening, but as some of the church leaders watched the body, they saw some twitching of the stomach muscles.

Soon the corpse began to take short breaths. They called for a video camera and began to record the progress, while some of them began to massage his body. At 5:15 p.m., nearly 48 hours after his documented death, Pastor Daniel opened his eyes, sat up and asked for water. This is one of the most documented resurrections of modern times. The video is available from Reinhart Bonnke's ministry.

Dr. Guy Chevreau, whom I met on my first trip to Mozambique in November of 2004, had just written a book called *Turnings*. He had been with Heidi and Rolland Baker on numerous occasions by that time and had been exposed to a lot of miracles and had also heard many stories of the dead being raised.

On pages 53 and 54 of *Turnings*, Dr. Chevreau relates his findings regarding resurrections that had already occurred in those days before the year 2004. He met Supresa (Surprise) Sithole, the international director of Iris Ministries under Heidi and Rolland Baker, as well as Florinda Tanueque, the wife of a pastor, who then supervised over sixty-nine churches.

At that time Supresa had witnessed one resurrection. Since then, he has seen two more people raised from the dead. One of these was just a young girl. As he held her hand and prayed for her, she suddenly squeezed his finger. It startled him and he jumped in shock. She was totally restored and he also recovered quickly from the shock, extremely excited about what God had done.

Florinda Tanueque had at that time raised three people from the dead, but before the year was up, I know the number had grown to four, according to a more recent report by Heidi Baker. I also was privileged to meet Florinda and her husband at a conference in Pemba. What an anointing they both carried!

The first person raised through the ministry of Florinda was a three-month-old baby girl. A victim of cholera and the resulting dehydration, she was revived and is still alive and healthy today. A few months after the first resurrection, a five-year-old girl, who had died of malaria, was brought to Florinda's house because the parents had heard about the first resurrection. She was also brought back to life. The third person raised was a middle-aged woman who had died of malaria. She was already stiff as were the first two.

Florinda explained to Dr. Chevreau what she had done for all three of the resurrections. On page 54 of *Turnings* we read:

Florinda was praying for each of the corpses while washing their bodies, in preparation for their funerals. Each time she prayed both in her mother tongue, Makua, and in tongues for twenty or thirty minutes speaking life into the corpses. Each time she noticed the body's chest rise as breath returned. Then the corpses' heads would move a little, side to side, as if saying "No" to death.

She didn't want to give any more details, but to say that yes, it has changed things markedly. They have led over 4,300 Muslims to Jesus over the last two years and planted eighty churches, largely because of these miracles.

Florinda did mumble a bit of an aside—because of the reports that have gone throughout the town and surrounding villages, people come to their house, day and night, with the sick and dying.

Dr. Chevreau later met Florinda's brother-in-law Pastor Jorge. He had one hundred and fifty churches under his care and had planted eight new ones in 2003.

Jorge had been used by God to raise seven people from the dead. He shared some details from the first five cases, and then it was obvious that he was tired of retelling the stories. He found it strange that a Christian "man of God" from the west was that interested in something that was so normal to him.

A more recent report comes from Rolland and Heidi Baker regarding a young man on their team who was beaten to death by a group of young thugs who were trying to disturb a meeting. He had gone over to the fringe of the crowd to try to calm them down, but they turned on him, beat him up and left him for dead.

One of the young thugs was captured and the police asked Rolland and Heidi to press charges against him. They refused to press charges, choosing rather to forgive him. This totally frustrated the authorities.

The body of the young team member had already been processed from the hospital to the morgue, but when the Bakers refused to press charges, the pneuma of the dead man returned to his body, causing quite a stir among the morticians.

The rest of the story is just as exciting. The resurrected young man went to the jail to forgive and release the one who helped to kill him, leading him to salvation in Jesus. This was just before Easter and he was able to attend the Easter service, as a powerful object lesson of Jesus' resurrection power.

This resurrection was certainly a different type than the others, in that no one was there to touch or breathe life into the corpse. The saints, however, were praying and knew that God could raise him from the dead. The apparent key to this resurrection was forgiveness. Forgiveness, obviously, is a means of breathing life into something that is dead.

The two authors that I have quoted in this chapter also report that the dead have been raised in many different ways. Prayer is usually involved, along with the laying on of hands. In one case, Bibles were laid on the victim's chest, and in many cases people prayed in tongues. In another case, the spirit of death manifested itself as a very dark person, but when it was rebuked and sent away, the dead returned back to life. As we recorded above, Florinda spoke life into each of the corpses that she saw restored to life.

Obviously, God is not as concerned with the method as He is with the relationship that comes from intimacy with Him. Intimacy produces obedience and releases an impartation of divine strategy.

Throughout this book we have been discovering some of the patterns in Scripture that make it clear that we can transfer life from the living to the dead. The normal means of doing this is by physical contact or by speaking or prophesying life into the corpse.

But God does not like being put in a box, and He can authorize us to do things that were never done in

Scripture. Jesus, Himself did a few very unusual things like spitting to make clay to put in a blind man's eyes, forgiving sins before he healed the sick and writing in the sand when religious leaders asked His opinion.

What we really must do (which Heidi and Rolland Baker would certainly verify) is to become so intimate with Jesus that we can recognize His voice in a crowd of voices. That deep intimacy will make us willing to do anything and everything that He asks us to do, no matter how strange it may seem to us or others. We will perform for a crowd of One, no matter where we are. And we will see all the miracles that He is ready and willing to do through us.

Spiritual Resurrections

As exciting as it will be for us to see the physically dead revived, especially if it is someone that we dearly love, we should all be just as excited or more so whenever God raises someone that is spiritually dead back to life. Spiritual resurrections can take many shapes and forms. I would refer to first-time decisions for Christ as spiritual resurrections, because every person was created in the image of God, even though that image was contaminated by Adam's fall.

Another form of spiritual resurrection takes place when a believer is touched by God and becomes aware of a whole new dimension of life in the Spirit. Suddenly, they discover that there is a whole lot more to this walk with God than they have been told. The life of the Holy Spirit transforms them in many ways, and they become incredibly fruitful, instead of being just religious and unfruitful.

A third category of spiritual resurrection is the return of a wayward child to the arms of the Father. People who have entered into the life of Jesus and then wandered back into the world can also be resurrected by the power of the Pneuma of God.

Examples of these three types of spiritual resurrections abound in our churches and ministries, so a lot of examples are not necessary. But to stimulate your desire for more, at least one example of each type is given.

Simple Prophetic Word Brings Eternal Life to Calgary Gal

One of the most exciting stories from our recent years of ministry took place in Calgary, Alberta, Canada. Cheryl lived in a very humble neighborhood and was invited by a gal named Dianne, a humble evangelist, to a home where we were to speak to a few of her friends. We ended up in a low-ceiling basement with about six or seven young adults, some of whom were chain smoking, including Cheryl, who was quite nervous about her encounter with us. Our ministry is kind of hard to describe to non-believers, and we have no idea what Dianne had told them about us.

We were there with very little of the warm spiritual atmosphere that we were used to. Dianne played a few old hymns on her guitar, which the young folk tried to sing. The thick cloud of cigarette smoke was a poor substitute for the glory cloud we have sensed in other ministry settings, but God was up to something special.

We prophesied destiny and purpose into each of their lives. When we ministered to Cheryl, Brenda looked her in the eyes, and with God's love flowing through her, she said to Cheryl, "God really loves you!" She added a few other details, but Cheryl was overwhelmed with those four words, which had never been spoken to her before by anyone.

The Holy Pneuma had breathed upon her through the words that Brenda had spoken to her. Her life began to be transformed from that day on. It didn't happen all at once, but she immediately became an evangelist, bringing friends and family to the church where we were ministering.

The next time we showed up in that church, she was still going strong in the Lord and she was being baptized. The following trip we witnessed a public marriage proposal in the Sunday evening service. A young man she had helped to find God was now asking her to marry him. Later we witnessed the wedding.

A few days ago, Cheryl wrote to us that she was now leading the ladies' ministry, and her husband was leading the men's ministry in the church. Both of them had won the battle with cigarettes and other personal challenges, and they were excited about the way that God was using them.

We are happy that we were obedient to go to that little basement where our clothes took on the smell of cigarettes, where we had to overcome the fear and curiosity of unsaved people, and where no love offering was taken to help us with our expenses. We love the way that Jesus breathes through us when we are yielded to Him.

Real Estate Broker Radically Transformed

Lisa Bourland is a very successful owner of two real estate businesses. She has won a top national award from the ERA real estate network. She had been raised in a strong evangelical denominational church in her Kentucky town where she and her parents had grown up. Lisa had been taught that God did not do miracles any more and that since we now have the Bible, we don't need to see the things that were reported in the Bible.

Lisa was taught that the power of the Holy Spirit was replaced by the teachings of the Bible. But of course, they were not to try to duplicate what happened in the Bible, and they needed to remember that some of the teachings, especially concerning spiritual gifts, were not really valid anymore.

But God had plans for Lisa, and He sent to her town a fiery revival evangelist named Vance Murphy, who believed everything that Lisa had been taught not to believe. Not only did he believe it, but he had experienced much of it and practiced it regularly. Through divinely-arranged circumstances, Lisa found herself in one of the meetings. After observing the power of prophetic knowledge and the miracles that were happening, Lisa's theology began to undergo a radical transformation, and she developed a passionate hunger for more of Jesus and His power.

Before long, with no religious framework for it, she found herself in Mozambique with Vance's team, meeting Heidi Baker, going to church at the garbage dump, getting firsthand experience in delivering someone from demonic power, seeing amazing miracles and being healed herself of severe hearing loss. Lisa was wrecked forever. She could never go back to her past religious way of living. Resurrection life had been imparted to her in an amazing way.

Lisa has spent a large percentage of her time in the last two years or so, going to the mission fields that God has opened up to her. With Vance, she has co-led the Father's House Ministry, establishing orphan homes in several countries. She has also established a ministry base in her home town in Kentucky, where she hosts a House of Prayer and influences many people, especially the youth of her town.

When we came to her home town a few months ago, doors opened in her former non-Pentecostal church for us and our House of Prayer worship team. The youth pastor, with about eighty youth, was desperate to know how to take them deeper in God. Gothic youth were now coming to his youth group and he felt totally inadequate.

We were blessed with the unusual opportunity of ministering prophetically with our teams to about sixty evangelical young people and their leaders. They will never ever be the same again. We were told that the kids kept asking each other, "What did the prophets say to you?" They all had cassette tapes of the words and they listened to them over and over again. The leaders have had a new boldness to go after the power of God in their lives and their church. Both the youth leader and the church's worship leader visited Lisa's prayer room and were filled with the Holy Pneuma. Who knows what will happen next!

It all began with a young man, who had the Pneuma of God flowing through him. Because he had the life of God in him, he was able to transfer this life to a gal who didn't even believe in it. Resurrection life can trump the power of death every time.

Wayward Children Return to Father

We probably all know of many prodigals that have returned to God because someone was in the right place at the right time with the right words from the Holy Pneuma of God.

I can think of a gal who didn't want to have anything to do with us, but Jesus brought her across our path, and she was confronted with the love of Jesus, not just once or twice, but several times. She yielded more and more each time and returned to the love of her Heavenly Father, to the great joy of her earthly parents, who are special friends of ours. Now she is a passionate worshipper and has a wonderful relationship with Jesus and her family.

I can think of a pastor's son who disliked the pressure of being different from other kids. He wanted more sports and adventure than his parents thought was appropriate and he quit church when he was free to do so. His life became involved with many activities that grieved his parents. When strong prophetic words of destiny were given to him on several occasions, he began to re-evaluate his life and desires. He now has a special relationship with his Heavenly Father and knows he has an important Kingdom destiny.

I can think of another young man who was steadily drifting away from God during his teen years. His mother prayed fervently for him and his brother. God kept speaking to his heart, but he would close his ears to the voice of God. Finally, with a feeling of emptiness in his soul, he agreed to attend a meeting we were holding and then consented to come forward for ministry.

The word the Lord gave him ministered to his heart the hope and destiny that he so desperately needed. He had been nervous about receiving a word and fearful that his past would be exposed, but he received nothing but love and the awareness that God had an awesome purpose for his life. He was to become a leader in the Kingdom of God and his spirit confirmed it.

His life was immediately turned around after he received the word. Shortly after graduating from high school, he joined the military and was sent to Afghanistan. There he quickly began a Bible Study group, teaching and mentoring many other soldiers. He is a bold young man sharing the gospel every chance he gets. He will soon be on his way to Special Forces training, expecting to have many more opportunities to share the love of Jesus. And his journey has just begun. He is another example of what God can do when we allow Him to breathe on dry bones.

Over the last few years of ministry, we have seen hundreds of saints who were living in varying degrees of spiritual death or paralysis become activated and revived by the Pneuma of God, as we faithfully listened to the voice of God and delivered the words He instructed us to share. What a joy it is to see the pneuma of the person revived and to see them once again walking in the joy of their Lord!

We are now going to look at how you can take the principles and truths that we have learned in this study of resurrections and apply them in very practical ways to your own life and ministry. Don't quit reading now. The most important chapter is still ahead.

Chapter 10

Life and Death Applications

We are all involved in this incredible invisible warfare that goes on in billions of battlefronts around the world every day. People are being shot down, crippled and removed from active duty all the time, and it seems that almost no one is coming to help them. Some have been given up for dead and left to rot on the battlefield, while others have been prepared for their final resting places by spiritual morticians. The battleground is littered with spiritual corpses and the graveyards are filled to capacity.

It's time for those who have the Holy Pneuma residing within them to rise up into their destinies as life givers and invite Him to flow through them to touch others. Their fellow soldiers are wounded and dying and waiting for the touch that transfers life from the living to the dead. They are waiting for someone who has the breath of life within them to breathe that breath into their nostrils as God did to Adam and Eve.

Physical Resurrections

Although most of the applications of this book involve spiritual resurrections, we should not forget that God has also given us the power and authority to raise the physically dead. It is not just for a few super-spiritual people or just for the people overseas. Frequent resurrections will happen right here in the western world and will increase in the next few years. Many children and youth will be involved in these resurrections.

Only those who disqualify themselves will be disqualified. Remember the chapter entitled "Who Can Raise the Dead?" Be alert and listening for the promptings God will give you at the right time and place.

Our friend Lisa, whom we talked about in the last chapter, is already going after opportunities to see the dead raised. She had an opportunity recently, but she was not allowed to get close to the corpse because the man was murdered and the police were investigating. However, Lisa had another person hold a cell phone to the dead man's ear while she prayed and prophesied life into him. He didn't revive, but she will keep praying and speaking life until she has seen the dead raised.

To Raise the Dead, Remember the Following

1. If you have life you can give it.
2. The Holy Pneuma in you is the same Holy Pneuma that was in Peter and Paul when they raised the dead.
3. Life can be transferred through your hands or your body, as well as through objects that you have touched or worn.
4. Life can be breathed into dead bodies to bring them back to life.
5. Prophetic words that come from the Holy Pneuma convey life from God.
6. When you are listening and hearing God, obey what He says, even when He tells you to command a dead body to arise.
7. You will never feel ready or spiritual enough to raise the dead, so don't wait until you do.
8. There may be times when you need to be alone with the body.
9. Don't give up too quickly. Some resurrections have come after hours of prayer and warfare.
10. Give God all the glory and worship Him for the privilege of being a carrier of His living Pneuma.

Spiritual Resurrections

If we are walking in close fellowship with Jesus and pursuing intimacy with Him, then we will become much more aware of the opportunities that He will give us to breathe His life into others and touch them in a way that revives them again. There are many times that we take just a small or minor hit that takes some of the love, joy and peace away from our hearts. We are not walking away from God, but we are not at our best in His service during these times.

When we are not walking in the fullness of the Fruit of the Spirit, we are not as useful to God. That is when we need a gentle word from another saint who sees with the eyes of the Spirit and hears His voice. Their inspired words can quickly counteract the hit that carried the spirit of death and revive us with the Spirit of Life.

Words that bring discouragement, weariness of the soul and feelings of failure are diseases that can plague us as Christians. Words that bring encouragement, refreshing and confidence in God are medicines that counteract the negative words. They are also vitamins for the spirit of a man, giving him victory over the diseases of the soul and also the energy to live and work for the Lord.

As I write this, I feel inspired to emphasize as much as I can that the Lord really, really wants to use you to raise the dead. He wants you to know that you do not need to wait until you feel you have your own act together. That's when He will NOT be able to use you! Let Him use you today while you are still aware of all your "stuff" that you don't like. Let Him use you to help someone else that feels like you do, and tell them that God loves them just the way they are.

You will get so blessed raising up the downcast souls and spirits of men, women, and children that you will become addicted to the experience. And as you are faithful in the little things, God will give you more and more authority and responsibility. And before you know it, others will be ministering life to you when you are down, and you will find your "stuff" becoming less and less of a problem to you.

Beloved of God, please understand the depth of God's love for you! May this little book become the Breath of Life—the Pneuma of God for your own soul and spirit. You have taken a lot of hits, which were never countered by the ministry of spiritual healing, through another child of God. You have learned to function in spite of the pain, but you are not fulfilling your potential because the pain has actually drained away a portion of your spiritual energy to keep it under cover.

Right now you can allow the Spirit of Life who inspired me to write this book to flow through you and heal your own soul and spirit. By doing that you will free up space in your heart's "hard drive" for more downloads from Heaven. Just pray this prayer:

Holy Spirit, please breathe into me Your breath of life to erase from my spirit the pain of my past experiences, even those that happened just today. Please fill me with Your life and love for others and breathe Your breath of life through me into their hearts. Open my eyes to see their needs. Open my ears to hear Your promptings, and give me the will to obey without the fear of man.

I renounce that spirit of fear, and receive freely the Spirit of Love, Power and a Sound Mind, in Jesus name. Amen.

If you prayed that prayer, expect things to change in your life. Expect God to show you more and more people who need reviving. Some may need just a little shot of oxygen, and some may need to be placed in "intensive care" for some time. The Holy Spirit will lead you and guide you. Others will be there to help teach and train you when you need it the most.

Don't quit if you feel like you missed it and said the wrong thing, etc. You won't always get it right the first time. Just stay humble and ask the Holy Spirit to give you more wisdom and revelation. Pray for more details and accuracy. Pray for your eyes to see and for your ears to hear with more clarity and precision than ever before. Keep asking God to take you to a new level, going from glory to glory. Never become complacent or satisfied with the status quo.

God is pleased with such prayers, unless you are seeking glory for yourself. To circumvent the natural tendency to desire to look good in the eyes of man, ask God to search your heart and reveal your impure motives. Confess them and ask Him to download more of His own heart. He always responds to that kind of prayer and will continue to take you deeper into the vastness of His own heart.

May God take us all deeper into His heart, and may we all enjoy the adventure of bringing resurrection life to the dead and dying. And may His love surround us and protect us as we help Him raise up His mighty army on the earth.

BEN R. PETERS

With over 40 years of ministry experience, Ben Peters with his wife, Brenda, have been called to an international apostolic ministry of equipping and activating others. As founders and directors of Open Heart Ministries, Ben and Brenda have ministered to tens of thousands with teaching and prophetic ministry. The result is that many have been saved, healed, delivered and activated into powerful ministries of their own.

Ben has been given significant insights for the body of Christ and has written fourteen books in the past ten years, since beginning a full-time itinerant ministry. His passions and insights include unity in the body of Christ, accessing the glory of God, five-fold team ministry, prophetic ministry, and signs and wonders for the world-wide harvest.

Kingdom Sending Center
P.O. Box 25
Genoa, IL 60135

www.KingdomSendingCenter.org
ben.peters@kingdomsendingcenter.org

"The Ultimate Convergence is imminent and I am excited with all that God is going to do." ~ Dr. C. Peter Wagner

BEN R. PETERS

The Ultimate Convergence
An End Times Prophecy of the Greatest
Shock and Awe Display Ever to Hit Planet Earth
by Ben R. Peters

Available from Kingdom Sending Center
www.kingdomsendingcenter.org

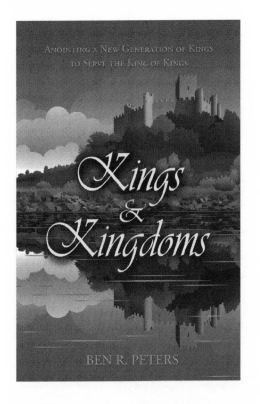

Kings and Kingdoms
Anointing a New Generation of Kings
to Serve the King of Kings
by Ben R. Peters

Available from Kingdom Sending Center
www.kingdomsendingcenter.org

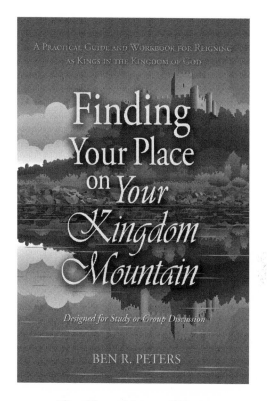

**Finding Your Place
on Your Kingdom Mountain**
A Practical Guide and Workbook for Reigning
as Kings in the Kingdom of God
by Ben R. Peters

Designed for Study or Group Discussion

Available from Kingdom Sending Center
www.kingdomsendingcenter.org